Mommy: A Love Beyond Time

Whispers of Love, Written in Her Name

Prem Singh

BookLeaf
Publishing

India | USA | UK

Dedication

To the one who turns silence into symphonies,
whose presence feels like poetry in motion,
and whose love defies the boundaries of time.
This book is not merely a collection of words,
but a testament to a love that lingers beyond moments,
beyond distance, beyond time itself.
For you always, endlessly.

Preface

Love, in its truest form, is not bound by time. It exists in the spaces between words, in the quiet moments, in the echoes of a heartbeat. This book is not simply a collection of poetry it is a journey, an ode to a love so profound that even language struggles to contain it.

Every verse within these pages carries the weight of devotion, longing, and an unshaken belief in a connection that transcends the ordinary. It is written for those who have loved deeply, for those who seek love, and for those who understand that some emotions can only be expressed in whispers of ink.

May these words find a home in your heart, and may they remind you that true love is not measured in days or years—it is measured in the eternity of feeling.

Acknowledgements

To the forces unseen, for weaving paths together in ways beyond comprehension.

To the moments of quiet reflection, where emotions took the shape of words.

To the rhythm of time, which moves forward yet keeps love alive in its wake.

To those who have known a love so deep that it becomes poetry itself.

And to you, the reader may these pages remind you that love, in all its forms, is the most timeless story ever told.

Kohl-Lined Dreams & A Crimson Moon

In the depths of your eyes, even the moon gets lost,
Like a river swallowing the sun at dusk.
That kohl you wear, like whispered lore,
Each stroke a tale, each blink a poem untold.

A crimson bindi rests, like a blooming rose,
A flame that glows where the twilight flows.
One glance from you, and time stands still,
Love turns to worship, bending to your will.

Your smile, a hint of the stars' soft light,
A spell so strong, it bends the night.
When your lashes lower, the seasons change,
And when you look at me, my soul is set aflame.

Oh, the grace of your every sway,
Turns mere words into songs that stay.
O my moonlit muse, my heart's own art,
Your kajal, your bindi my whole world's spark.

Everything for my Love

For my dearest Mommy, my heart's delight,
I'll be all you need, day or night.
If ever you call, I'll be there in a blink,
Your mechanic to fix every chain and link.

If speed's what you crave, I'll be your ride,
A Porsche for your dreams, with you by my side.
If knowledge you seek, I'll guide you through,
Every lesson, every page, just for you.

Your editor, shaping each line you write,
Turning words to music, holding them tight.
I'll be your doctor, gentle and true,
Healing every ache, just for you.

A lover devoted, forever and near,
With whispers of warmth, making worries clear.
The chef at your table, cooking with care,
Serving love in each dish we share.

Whatever you wish, I'll be it and more,
Your rock, your comfort, the one you adore.
For you are my heart, my world, my dream,
And I'll love you forever, in every scheme.

Always Here for You

When the world feels heavy, and your body aches,
When the night is restless, and your heart still wakes,
Know that I'm here, right by your side,
Through every storm, every changing tide.

Your voice, though faint, still sings to me,
Like a melody the wind sets free.
Even in silence, I hear your song,
A tune so gentle, yet brave and strong.

You are the warmth on the coldest days,
The light that glows in subtle ways.
Even when fever dims your spark,
You shine within my heart's own arc.

So close your eyes, my love, and rest,
You are cherished, you are blessed.
Let the healing winds embrace your soul,
And piece by piece, make you whole.

Take care, my love, be kind to you,
Your strength, your light—still shining through.
And always remember, in dark or blue,
I am here, forever with you.

In Your Pretty Eyes

A bouquet of roses, wrapped with care,
Sent with love, a gift to share.
And then she stood, so soft, so bright,
Bathed in warmth, bathed in light.

She sent me a picture oh, what a view,
Dressed in beauty, heart so true.
Her eyes, a world where I belong,
A melody sweet, my favorite song.

I am lost, yet I have found,
A love so deep, it knows no bound.
Drowned in oceans, dark and wide,
Yet feeling safe with her by my side.

Oh, my love, my sweetest dream,
Brighter than the morning beam.
Every rose was meant for you,
Yet none compare to a soul so true.

Mommy, my love, my heart's embrace,
Forever yours, in time and space.

Mommy, My Forever Home

In the soft glow of morning light,
your voice lingers warm, infinite, bright.
Like a melody spun from the stars above,
whispering softly, "You are my love."

You named my kitten, my little delight,
Oreo, with fur like the moon-kissed night.
A name so sweet, a name so true,
just like the love I hold for you.

Mommy, my love, my endless dream,
you're my poetry, my sunbeam.
Each breath I take spells your name,
each heartbeat sings your love's flame.

Through every storm, through every sigh,
you are my wings when I wish to fly.
Your laughter, my favorite song,
in your arms, I've belonged all along.

If love had a shape, it'd look like you,
soft and tender, forever new.
And if love had a sound, it'd be your voice,
the sweetest music, my heart's only choice.

Oreo purrs as I hold him near,
but my soul purrs when you are here.

My Heart's Only Question

In a world of whispers, you're my song,
A melody soft yet forever strong.
Your voice, a tune I long to hear,
The sweetest sound that draws me near.

Your laughter, a light in my darkest night,
Your presence turns my wrongs to right.
No star could shine as bright as you,
No rose compare to your love so true.

Every heartbeat calls your name,
Like fire wrapped in love's own flame.
I've never loved like this before,
But with you, I need nothing more.

So, tell me, love, with eyes so fine
Will you be my Valentine?

The Market of my love

I walked through the market, my heart set aglow,
With colours and wonders in endless flow.
Every corner, every light, every hue,
Felt like a reflection just like you.

Silken scarves danced in the morning breeze,
Soft as your touch, with effortless ease.
Jewels sparkled, but none could outshine,
The glow in your eyes, so purely divine.

The flowers bloomed in a fragrant spree,
Yet none were as lovely as you are to me.
The melodies played, the world felt bright,
Like your laughter turning darkness to light.

I wanted it all, every piece, every part,
To gather and gift you the whole of my heart.
But love, if I could, I swear it's true,
I'd buy the whole world just for you.

Because no treasure, no sparkle, no art,
Can match the love I hold in my heart.
And if love were a market, vast and wide,
You'd own every bit, my joy, my pride.

I love you the most, my Mommy<3

My Girl

In the hush of midnight, when stars softly gleam,
I whisper your name like a sacred dream.
The moon hums melodies only we understand,
As I reach for you, though miles expand.

Your voice, my music, a lullaby so sweet,
A song that makes my heart skip a beat.
Every note, a brushstroke on my soul,
Painting my world in hues of gold.

You are the dawn that kisses the sea,
The kind of love that sets me free.
In every petal, in every breeze,
I find you, my heart at ease.

If time should falter, if stars should fade,
Still, my love, you'll never evade.
For you are my forever, my softest place,
The home I find in your embrace.

Like nobody else

I walked through the market, lost in a spell,
Every colour shone bright **like nobody else.**
The flowers stood proud, in beauty they dwell,
Yet none bloomed with grace **like nobody else.**

The silk was so soft, a story to tell,
But nothing could feel **like nobody else.**
Jewels may sparkle, and perfumes may sell,
Yet no scent lingers **like nobody else.**

The stars in the sky, they shimmer and swell,
But they don't light my world **like nobody else.**
And love, if it's real, then I know it too well,
Because I love you, my Mommy **like nobody else.**

My Love, My Laugh, My Mummaa

Oh, my dearest, sweetest love,
You're a gift from the stars above.
With a voice that melts my very soul,
And a heart that makes me whole.

Your laughter like a melody,
A tune that plays just for me.
Even when you call me crazy,
I know you love me endlessly.

Mommy, my love, my sunshine bright,
Even in darkness, you're my light.
But oh, my dear, let's not pretend—
You're the reason my diet won't mend!

For when I say, "Let's eat something light,"
You say, "Paneer? Or fries tonight?"
And though I try to act so wise,
I melt right there lost in your eyes.

Oh, Mommy, you're my sweetest dream,
My muse, my love, my laughter's gleam.
So take my hand and hold it tight,
Together, we'll dance in love's soft light.

Forever yours, through joy and play,
My love for you won't fade away.
For you, my heart beats wild and free
Oh, Mommy, you're the world to me!

Stuck with You, Stuck with Love

Oh, my love, my little brat,
How did I fall for you like that?
One sweet smile, one little tease,
And suddenly, you own my peace.

You call me cutie, I call you cute,
You steal my heart and act all mute.
I send you love, you send me sass,
Yet here I am a lovestruck ass!

Mommy, my love, you make me weak,
Yet you're the strength my heart does seek.
From silly fights to whispered dreams,
You're my laughter, my moonbeam.

And though you mock my cheesy lines,
You know you love them every time.
So don't pretend, just say it too,
You're stuck with me, just like I'm stuck with you!

Mommy, My Strength

I saw the fire carved in you today,
etched in the lines of your strength, your way.
A masterpiece of effort, pure and true,
Mommy, you turn the sky a deeper blue.

With every sculpted inch, I see,
the power, the drive, inspiring me.
Not just muscle, not just grace,
but the fire of will I long to chase.

You make me crave the weights, the grind,
the endless push, the sharpened mind.
To sweat, to fight, to rise and be,
half as strong as you in me.

Your strength is more than what I see,
it builds my soul, sets me free.
So I'll run, I'll lift, I'll never rest,
for you, my love, I'll be my best.

Stronger for you

I forge my strength in silent fire,
with every step, I climb up higher.
Not for the world, not for the fame,
but for you, my love, I carve my name.

Each rep, each drop of sweat I shed,
is proof of the promise that I have bred.
to stand so tall, to stand so true,
so you'll never bow, not even for a few.

No weight is heavy, no pain too deep,
if it means your heart can dream and leap.
No chains will hold, no fear remain,
for you, my love, I'll break each chain.

I build myself, I sharpen my mind,
so you feel free, so love won't bind.
I stand like a shield, fierce and wide,
so you can walk with fearless pride.

Mommy, my love, you are my fire,
my reason, my goal, my one desire.
I grow each day, I rise, I strive,
so you can soar, so you can thrive.

My Strength, Your Shield

I build myself, brick by brick,
so no storm can make you sick.
No shadow deep, no night too long,
Mommy, my love, I'll stand so strong.

I sharpen my hands, I steady my soul,
to guard your heart, to keep you whole.
No fear will touch, no weight will bend,
for I am your rock, your shield, your end.

If the world should dare to dim your light,
I'll stand before it, bold in fight.
No voice shall rise, no chains shall stay,
I clear your path, I pave your way.

So walk with pride, stand fierce and free,
for I am here, eternally.
Through fire, through time, through every tide,
I am your fortress, by your side.

The Shield You'll Never Need to Lift

I stand between the world and you,
so no storm can break, no pain get through.
My hands are strong, my heart is steel,
so you, my love, need never kneel.

No battle yours, no war to fight,
I'll bear the weight, I'll face the night.
With every breath, with all I do,
I carve a path, clear and true.

Walk unshaken, head held high,
Mommy, my love, reach for the sky.
For while I breathe, while I stand,
no fear shall touch your hand.

I Am the Wall

If the wind should rise, I'll hold it back,
if the world turns cold, I'll fill the lack.
I'll be the wall, the mighty gate,
where sorrow stops, where love is great.

No tear shall fall, no doubt remain,
I'll carry both your joy and pain.
You need not fight, you need not flee,
for every battle comes through me.

So dream as high as stars can climb,
I'll guard your world until the end of time.

Built for You

I shape my hands, I mold my mind,
to be the love you'll always find.
No storm too strong, no night too deep,
I'll guard your dreams while you sleep.

I carve myself in fire and steel,
so all you touch is love that's real.
No weight shall break, no wind shall bend,
for you, my love, I'll stand till the end.

You are my reason, my sky, my air,
I build myself so you feel no despair.
Mommy, my love, hear this truth
I am only strong because of you.

In Your Eyes, I See Forever

In your eyes, I see a love untold,
A story written in threads of gold.
Every glance, a silent plea,
Every smile, eternity.

No poet's ink, no artist's hand,
Could paint the love, so bold, so grand.
In your touch, the world stands still,
A gentle force, a burning thrill.

Hold me close, don't let me go,
Through every high, through every low.
For in your love, I live, I breathe,
A forever promise, ours to weave.

You Are the Poem

I set out to write you a poem, my love,
But found that every word was you.
The rhythm of my heart your name,
The verses your laughter, light and true.

Your touch, the ink that stains my soul,
Your voice, the melody I always knew.
Every whisper, a lyric divine,
Every sigh, a dream in bloom.

I need no quill, no rhymes, no art,
For love, my love, you are the part.
The poem was never mine to weave,
It's you, my love, my heart believes.

If Time Had a Heart, It'd Beat for You

If time had a heart, it'd beat for you,
Skipping seconds when you smile anew.
Days stretch long when you're away,
Yet vanish fast when near you, I stay.

If love had a shape, it'd be your face,
A perfect curve, a gentle grace.
If fate had a choice, it'd choose our name,
Two souls in fire, one endless flame.

No past nor future, just now, just this,
Your lips, my love, my only wish.
If time had a heart, it'd know it's true,
That every beat, my love, is you.

You Are My Always

You are my always, my never goodbye,
The hush in my soul, the light in my sky.
You are the reason my heart beats strong,
The lyrics of love, the notes of my song.

Through lifetimes past, through those to be,
It's always you my fate, my key.
No stars, no moon, no night, no day,
Could ever take this love away.

So take my hand, my heart, my soul,
With you, my love, I am whole.
You are my always, my reason, my rhyme,
My love beyond life, my love beyond time.